FINANCIAL
INDEPENDENCE
NO RISK, NO INCOME

AGBAI INA OBASI

FINANCIAL
INDEPENDENCE
NO RISK, NO INCOME

CITI OF
BOOKS

CITIOFBOOKS, INC.
3736 Eubank NE Suite A1
Albuquerque, NM 87111-3579
www.citiofbooks.com
Hotline: 1 (877) 389-2759
Fax: 1 (505) 930-7244

Ordering Information:

Quantity sales. Special discounts are available on quantity purchases by corporations, associations, and others. For details, contact the publisher at the address above.

Printed in the United States of America.

ISBN-13:   Softcover   978-1-959682-36-3
                      eBook   978-1-959682-37-0

Library of Congress Control Number: 2022920889

Author's Contact Details
Email Address: ina_obasi@yahoo.com
Contact Number: 91956217648

TABLE OF CONTENTS

DEDICATION

This book is dedicated especially to; my late father-Chief Ina E. Obasi [Ekwueme 1 of Abiriba] in continuation of his service to his community and humanity at large, my family and friends who inspired me to greater heights and ensuring the realization of this book.

ACKNOWLEDGMENTS

I wish to appreciate certain persons who were of great help to me while writing this book:

Firstly, I wish to thank God Almighty for keeping me alive and giving me the grace to write this book.

Kennedy Madu, who did the cover design and page layout. Samuel Ogoazi, who edited and proofread the book. Ireke Amoji, James and Nena.

My family, who made their own input at various stages in the project. And many other friends and relations who cannot be mentioned specifically because of space constraints

FOREWORD

Coming back to Nigeria in the mid-1980s after eight years in The United States, I was touched by the level of poverty prevalent in my Country. It was a tangible kind of poverty that could be seen and felt just by looking at the faces of most people everywhere in the country. Since then, it has been my strong desire to help as many people as possible come out of their predicament. This was the beginning of my vision to help people achieve Financial Independence and live better.
This book is the medium through which I hope to reach out to people, share my experiences with them and achieve this noble objective.

I am a firm believer that God created every individual unique. Unfortunately, we have tended to move towards uniformity. This trend has created a major problem in our society making people behave like robots thereby giving rise to a high level of sycophancy among our people with its adverse consequences on our development.

Sycophancy: a "disease" which makes people hero-worship leaders even when they are clearly wrong is worse than Corruption. Sycophancy has turned the citizenry into a docile lot willingly accepting the atrocities committed by their leaders. This has created room for our leaders to massively abuse their entrusted positions and enrich themselves with impunity.

Only those who have learned th
power of sincere and selfless
contribution experience life's deepest
joy: true fulfillment.

Anthony Robbins

Encouraged by this widespread reverence and praise-singing towards their unacceptable behavior, our leaders persist in primitively accumulating wealth that they cannot exhaust in a lifetime. They forget that this world is only a transit point and not our destination.

A major cause of this abnormal behavior [sycophancy] is financial insecurity. Therefore, I believe that as more people become financially independent, the level of sycophancy among our people will be greatly minimized. Our leaders would then be held more accountable for their actions and adequate punishment meted out to erring ones. This will certainly sanitize the Private and Public sectors and bring sustainable development to our land. My reason for writing this book, therefore, is to inspire our people to think and act to achieve financially independent.

FINANCIAL INDEPENDENCE

The way to become financially
independent is to desire it fervently.
Desire is what best sustains our thoughts.
The more passionate your desire, the more
quickly the things you want will spring to your life…
In your time of desire, remember to be "still and know
that I am God"

Mark Fisher

A lot of people go through life broke because of their inability
to understand their finances. Consequently, being financially
independent is a decision everyone must take and pursue
vigorously. I have always sought an opportunity to help people
improve on their finances. I believe that as you read this book,
you will be challenged to take a decision that will change your
fortunes forever.

Setting Goals

Everyone dreams, but it's only those who take consistent action to actualize their dreams that get to live the dream. Setting a goal is the first step in turning your dream to reality.

You must understand why you are setting the goal and what is required to achieve the goal. To effectively do this, you must be sincere to yourself and evaluate your strengths and weaknesses, starting from your base and seeking out ways to improve on your weaknesses.

Passion is the key that drives the process. The more passionate you are in setting and pursuing the goal, the better chances you must achieve it. It is recommended that the goal be shared with loved ones for effective buy-in and support. The goal should also be in writing, specific with details, measurable and challenging. Challenging goals improve productivity and induce a high-performance culture that helps to achieve success.

Without setting a goal, it's very difficult to achieve success. But just setting the goal is not enough, you must take immediate and consistent action to achieve the goal. To illustrate how important setting a goal is, a Harvard study showed that college students that set goals just before their graduation achieved 10 times more than their counterparts, after ten years of graduation.

Once you set the goal, begin to adjust your mind to envision the success of it [financial independence]. Begin to feel the joy of achieving the goal and abhor the pain of failure. One of the first things we must do is to shift our paradigm. This entails thinking outside our present circumstances. A lot of people do not understand the power of setting goals. They are afraid of venturing outside their comfort zones. However, they forget that whenever progress is made in any field of human endeavor it had been accompanied by change. Change is the only thing that is constant but always comes with uncertainty and risk. If we fear taking risks, we shall most likely remain the same and end up not achieving much in life.

Therefore, we must learn to take risks. Remember, *NO RISK NO INCOME*. Once we accept this, we are on our way to financial independence.

> Setting goals is the first step in turning the
> Invisible to visible, the foundation of all success—
> All goal setting must be immediately followed by
> both the development of a plan, and massive and
> consistent action towards its fulfillment.

> Anthony Robbins

With this brief overview, let me share my experiences in the pursuit of financial independence illustrated with living examples drawn from my interactions with people with respect to various aspects of investments.

The Year 1986.

Early in life, I developed the belief that leaders
are readers. Book could take me to other lands
where I could meet unique people like Abraham
Lincoln or Ralph Waldo Emerson whom I could
utilize as my personal coaches.

Anthony Robbins

I graduated from Marquette University Law School in
Milwaukee, Wisconsin in 1986 and was called to the Bar in
the state of Wisconsin before rushing back to Nigeria with high
hopes in the same year.
I had dreamt of becoming the Attorney General of the
Federation and consequently helping to shape our laws to
reflect the trend in the World then. That dream was never to
be as I was confronted with overwhelming challenges on the
Bench in particular, and the Judiciary in general. I refer to the
overwhelming and suffocating behavior of the Senior Advocates
of Nigeria [SAN] in the courtrooms including simple things
like seating arrangements; the unrepentant attitude of the
Judges towards the use of Stenographers, causing inefficient and
inaccurate reflections of the court records. The corrupt Police
and Judicial system, political, economic, and social insecurity
coupled with widespread hunger were a few of the constraints
that the system was grappling with. Thus, the efficient
functioning of the system was distorted making the desired
result of achieving an efficient legal system, unattainable.

The year 1986 also saw the devaluation of the Naira. The
exchange rate went from one Naira to the US Dollar to four
Naira to the Dollar after the introduction of the Structural
Adjustment Program [SAP]. When this book was first published
in 2009, the official exchange rate for the Naira was about

N150 to the dollar. Today [2022] the official currency exchange rate is more than N600 to the dollar. While I was able to buy more things with the few dollars I first came back with from the United States, the generality of Nigerians suffered untold hardship from the implementation of this ill-conceived SAP.

But my main reason for mentioning the year 1986 specifically is because that was the year, I moved into my brother's house in the Government Residential Area [GRA] Ogudu, a suburb of Lagos southwest Nigeria. The area was relatively uninhabited then even though Government had provided basic amenities like good roads, electricity, and portable water.

The cost of a plot of land in the Ogudu GRA then was about fifty-thousand naira. I did not have fifty thousand Naira then, but I could have raised it if that was my goal and I had focused on it. I did not understand the time-value of money then especially as it relates to Real Estate. In 2009, the cost of a plot of land in the Ogudu GRA was more than twenty million naira. You could just imagine what a plot of land in Ogudu GRA would be today.

AS A CEO

Invest in people…. Help them achieve
their full potentials; for people who feel
good about themselves produce
good results.

Kenneth Blanchard
Spencer Johnson

After graduating from Law School in Lagos and subsequent call to the Nigerian Bar Association, I proceeded to National Youth Service [a well-conceived program aimed at uniting the youth of the various ethnic groups in the country]. I served in the Nigerian Reinsurance Corporation after which I got a job with the help of my wife [then, my girlfriend] in the legal department of a bank. I spent four years in the Bank and rose to the position of deputy manager in 1992 before moving on to a new job.

When I joined the new Company, I was posted to a branch in one of the most notorious markets in Lagos- the Idumota market as a marketing officer. Never in my life had I been exposed to that kind of environment. I was contemplating resigning when my Branch Manager was recalled to the Head Office and the mantle of leading the Branch fell on me. I took the challenge and within a period of two years, I had transformed the small branch from a cash office to a full-fledged branch and a dependable source of cash supply for the bank.

From Idumota branch I was posted to the commercial department in the Head Office. After two years at the Head Office Unit, I was sent to Aba, a major commercial center in Eastern Nigeria to manage two branches simultaneously.

At the Aba branch, I was faced with a dwindling balance sheet caused by the seizure of a shipload of textile materials at the Calabar Port by the Nigerian Customs. Trading in this contraband item then was a very profitable venture for the key players in the business who boosted the branch balance sheet to an enviable state prior to the seizure of the goods and my arrival at the branch.

With more than eighty percent of the balance sheet size threatened, we had to come up with new ways to grow our business. It was in one of our branch strategy sessions that the now famous mass marketing for savings and other Demand Deposit Account [DDA] products were first introduced to the banking industry in Nigeria. The mass marketing for savings entailed aggressively canvassing for new accounts by going out into the marketplace, distributing handbills, and encouraging prospective account holders to open accounts on the spot.

To encourage many of the traders to open accounts with the bank, we had to reduce the minimum deposit required to open an account from five thousand to one-thousand five hundred Naira which was the norm in the industry then. We developed a process where we will collect all the information including the initial deposits from the prospective customers and will go back to the bank to process the account opening and return to the customers, their passbooks before the close of business the same day.

In less than one year, we turned the fortunes of the branch around and made it a clear leader in savings deposits throughout the company. That branch had the largest savings deposits in the bank. It was this high-performance track record that earned me the position of General Manager/Chief Executive Officer [CEO] of the Bank's subsidiary companies.

The challenges in the subsidiaries were different from the ones I had encountered in my other assignments. The subsidiaries were made up of three separate companies: a stock brokerage firm, an insurance brokerage firm, and a finance company. While the insurance brokerage firm was doing well comparatively, the other two were not, especially the stock brokerage firm.

When I assumed office, I had received a mandate from the management of the Bank to fire at least seventy-five percent of the existing work force in a restructuring plan of the subsidiaries. Suffice it to say that the three companies were turned around in less than two years with only one member of staff fired and two or three members of staff who resigned due to their inability to cope with the mounting workload. By the third year, we had turned the Subsidiaries' performance from a negative profit position to a profit before tax [PBT] level more than one-hundred-and-fifty million Naira.

A manager must set goals beforehand,
praise and reprimand immediately, specifically,
honestly and with true feelings. He must ask
brief, important questions; speak the simple truth;
laugh, work, and enjoy. Perhaps
most important of all, he should encourage
the employees to do the same.

Kenneth Blanchard
Spencer Johnson

How did we achieve this feat without financial assistance from the Bank? We did it through goal setting, teamwork, open communication, boosting staff morale, rewarding excellence and above all, leadership by example. It was, indeed, a clear manifestation of the role of leadership in any successful business. We started by budgeting, setting group and individual targets and providing the resources required to achieve the targets. A yearly increase in the salaries of members of staff by the board of the subsidiaries best illustrates our attempt to match the Bank's performance salary structure with the subsidiaries'. Each salary increase required a corresponding increase in the individual and group targets to fund such increase.

Another thing we did was to encourage our customers to borrow from the finance arm of the subsidiary and to invest the funds in shares through the stock brokerage firm. Thus, we were able to generate income from interest accruing from the loans and commissions from the purchase and sale of stocks. This product was readily received by a portion of our teeming customers - the Bank's staff.

Each Subsidiary staff had his or her goals and was responsible for achieving the said goal. Members of staff were trained in-house and by external facilitators. The result was phenomenal. On one occasion I had to forgo a course in South Africa because of what I felt would be the negative impact of attending such a high-profile course with the cost implications on the morale of my staff. The subsidiaries had just started making profit when the company gave the approval for me to attend the course. The expenses were supposed to have been borne by the Bank originally. However, the Bank realized that the subsidiaries had started making profit and decided that they [the subsidiaries] should foot the bill. I could not imagine putting such a heavy unbudgeted burden on the recovering subsidiaries just to improve my career prospects. So, I declined the course as a personal sacrifice.

It was in these subsidiaries that I was exposed to the world of stock. That experience is the single most valuable lesson that I learned in my entire career, and this book is a direct result of that experience. My greatest achievement as CEO was getting many of the Bank's staff to develop an interest in the stock market.

To achieve this, I visited the various regional offices of the Bank selling shares to otherwise ignorant staff. At one point, I wrote a provocative article in the Bank's newsletter just to draw the attention of members of staff to the investment opportunities available in the stock market. I vividly recall an article I wrote in the news-a letter upbraiding the Bank staff for spending their up-front payments on buying used cars and filling the company's parking lot with junk cars when they could invest in Stock and secure their future.

In another article, I gave them a vivid illustration of what two bankers did in the early 1990s with their up- front payments and the outcome ten years later. One of the bankers had bought a used Mercedes Benz car with his up-front payment, while the other bought First Bank shares with his. Ten years later, the staff who invested in stock was enjoying his capital appreciation, bonuses, and dividends while the staff who bought the Benz was struggling to maintain his dilapidated "Tokunbo" [Nigerian slang for used imported goods].

These stories touched many of the staff and created a new level of awareness in them and our stock brokerage firm benefited immensely as they began to respond positively.

Today, many millionaires have been raised from among the company's staff through stock market investments. I also helped a few of our traditional businessmen, who hitherto had focused only on one line of business [some of which were no longer as profitable as they used to be] to see the benefits of diversifying their investment portfolio.

By the time I left, the subsidiaries had become an important arm of the Bank, a major contributor its bottom line and a melting pot for the newcomer Management Team who started reaping from the sweat of the unsung hero of the subsidiaries.

The good thing was that for the first time, I was able to do what I love most; helping people become financially independent.

INVESTMENT OPPORTUNITIES

Savings

Financial security and independence are like
a three-legged stool resting on savings,
Insurance and investments.

Brian Tracy

Savings is simply generated when you live below your earnings. It entails distinguishing between your needs and your wants and making sacrifices today, for future security and perhaps, enjoyment. It is difficult to become financially independent without learning the habit of savings. That is why Financial Independence is like a three-legged stool resting on Savings, Insurance, and Investment.

If you do not learn to save when your income is small, it will be certainly difficult to save when your income increases. The reason is simple, the act of saving is a learned lifestyle/habit and not dependent on how much you make. That is the simple reason why you see so many lottery winners reverting to status quo few years after winning the lottery.

Therefore, if you want to be financially independent, decide today to pay yourself first when you receive your next paycheck by putting 10% of it into your savings account. You will be amazed that nothing much will change in your life pattern except that your savings account will be richer by 10%. As you start this savings journey, over a period, you will begin to enjoy the power of compound interest on your savings. Below is my experience with Savings.

After reading the Richest Man in Babylon in the early 1990s, I developed a savings formula. In our company, we had the opportunity to receive a portion of our salary up-front; usually paid at the beginning of the year. Saving was consequently easy for me. All I did was set aside my up-front payment at the beginning of the year in a special savings account. Although the Richest Man in Babylon prescribed saving at least ten percent of your earnings, by saving my up-front payment, I was able to save upwards of forty percent of my total earnings. This gave me a pool of funds to invest in other assets. For instance, the two-bedroom portion of my house was built entirely from my up-front savings over a period of a few years.

What is important here is developing the habit of saving. I once asked my driver to start saving a portion of his income. The response was the general excuse that his income was not enough. So, we agreed that every month he would give me ten percent of his salary which I deposited in a savings account I had opened for him. At the end of the first month of our experiment, I asked him how he managed to survive the month. This time, his response was very positive. With the money he saved over a period, he was able to settle down, rented a house, get married, and took care of his family.

A similar thing happened to a Youth Service Corp member in my department. In her own case, I advised her to live on the monthly salary she received from her place of primary assignment [The Bank] while she saved the stipend paid to her by the National Youth Service Corps. The result was astonishing. At the end of her Youth Service year, the value of her investment in the stock market was almost five-hundred-thousand naira. Taking heed of my advice, she purchased shares of United Bank for Africa [UBA] PLC at prices below fifteen naira per share from her savings. In 2007, UBA's share price was more than fifty naira per share. She is now a role model to her family and friends in investment matters.

Most people spend their youth working and saving a portion of their salaries. Upon retirement at a much older age, they begin to dabble to investments with little or no experience. Most of them fail, largely due to inexperience, or for lack of the concerted energy or drive required to achieve success in that field, or because they have been tricked by fraudsters. Remember the period we are most endowed by nature is in our youth. You must start early to invest your savings.

From the illustrations above, it is obvious that savings alone are insufficient if you want to be financially independent. You must invest those savings in more profitable portfolios and ventures.

If you want to make money,
go to where money is.

Kennedy

The three major investment opportunities available to us all are:

✓ Investment in Shares
✓ Investment in Real Estate
✓ Investment in your own business

Let me briefly discuss Insurance before going into the core investment opportunities.

INSURANCE:

There is no better way to protect your assets and loved ones against unforeseen circumstances than Insurance - Health, Life, Home, Car, College etc. Insurance reduces the financial risk and gives support when an unexpected event happens.
The need for Insurance cannot be overemphasized for the following:

-An unexpected illness may cost a fortune without health Insurance.

-Losses due to natural disasters, accidents, or burglaries may be expensive to replace.

-Loss of a loved one is more painful and complicated by bills without life insurance.

Therefore, Insurance is highly recommended not only because MAYHEM is everywhere but also to grow your financial assets. However, doing this second leg of growing your assets will require the services of a competent broker.

Investment in Stocks

Your wealth can only grow to the extent you do.

T. Harv Eker

Investments in this area require knowledge and skills. For instance, to invest in stocks, you need to have information on:

- The company of your interest.
- The management and the company's track record
- The year-end of the company and what they offered the previous year in dividends and or bonuses.
- The industry trend where the company belongs.
- The stock market industry terminology like the bear, the bull, script issue, bonus, dividend, bid, offer, capital appreciation, ex cum. Etc.
- The performance trend of the stock of your interest
- When the stock is high and when it is low; and what factors are responsible for the ups and downs?
- When to buy and when to sell. This requires that you have an entry and exit strategy.
- It's always advisable to use the services of a professional broker to guide you especially at the initial time.

Furthermore, you must also make some decisions as to the type of stock you want to invest in and how much to invest in each stock. Do you want to invest in penny stocks or diversify your portfolio? The answers to these questions depend on how much money you have, your experience in the market and your gut feelings. I have made and lost money in both penny and high-priced stocks.

Below are some Tips for Investing in the Stock Market:

-Invest long time. The longer your term, the lower your risk. A minimum of 5 years Is recommended.

-Do not sell your stock immediately after a downturn to partake in the rebound.

-Don't put all your eggs in one basket. Stacy Johnson recommends subtracting your age from 100 and putting no more than the resulting percentage of your long-term savings in Stock. For example, if you are 40 years, you can only invest 60% of your long-term savings in stock. Also, balance between growth and income.

-You have the Options to invest in Individual Company Stocks or in the Mutual Funds or both.

-Mutual Funds Lower your risks and hassle. It is a giant pool of investment either in Stock or Bond or both that is Managed by professionals who do the buying and selling. You should Avoid commission based financial advisers and use the Fees based ones whose fees is Dependent on the income you made from the investment. Mutual funds that trade on exchanges Are called Exchange Traded Fund (ETF).

-Systematic Investment. Recommended that you invest fixed amounts at regular intervals like monthly.So, you get to buy more when stocks are cheap and less when stocks are high or costly.

As a beginner, you must be able to do some calculations like Simple Interest and Return on Investment [ROI], dividend yield, Price Earnings [PE] ratio, earning per Share [EPS], Returns on Equity [ROE] etc. These calculations will help you in your decision to invest in one stock or the other. It is possible to have high-priced stocks which have low Returns on Investment (ROI) and vice versa. This means that a stock that has a high price per unit may have a low dividend payout thereby yielding relatively little to investors while a stock with a low price per unit may have a high percentage of its income paid to investors as dividends. Analyzing these fundamentals is strategic in stock market investments.

If you think education is expensive, try ignorance.

anonymous

I did not start playing big in the stock market until I saw one stock grow from under thirty naira to over one-hundred-and-sixty naira in about six months. As at the time of this writing the price of this stock is around sixty naira. So be warned that stock prices fluctuate. Sometimes you lose and some other times you gain. But whatever you do, endeavor to obtain personal knowledge of the stock market and or advice of a competent Stockbroker.

As a greenhorn in the stock market, I watched Julius Berger's stock slide from about forty-eight naira to thirty naira and decided that it was time to go in based on the scanty knowledge I had gleaned from reading stock market magazines. Soon after I bought the shares at thirty-one naira, the price started going up. I was excited. It got to forty-five naira per share but instead of selling, I got greedy expecting to double my investment in less than one month. While I was waiting, the Stock price crashed to below twenty naira per share and stayed there for a long time. I finally lost patience and sold at a loss. The price of Julius Berger stock in 2007 was more than fifty naira.

Another time I lost a substantial amount of money was a couple of years ago when Nigerian Breweries [NB] PLC declared a bonus of one-for-one at the end of its financial year. I had invested heavily in the stock, banking on the information I had received concerning the intended bonus. I had bought a substantial number of the shares at prices slightly above one-hundred naira per share. The projection was that the price would get up to one-hundred-and-thirty naira before it would be marked down and thereafter it would hover around seventy-five naira. The price did get up to the projected figure and was marked down around sixty-five naira.

Unfortunately, by this time, the Central Bank of Nigeria had just announced the bank consolidation policy. The banks were required by the new policy to recapitalize to the tune of twenty-five-billion naira [two-hundred million USD] or merge with others and thus achieve a cumulative share capital to that tune. The banks began to shop for funds to comply with this policy. These measures adversely affected the bank's aggregate funding in the Stock Market which in turn had a negative impact on prices of stocks in the Market and they came crashing. So, be aware that a seemingly unrelated government policy or pronouncement can have a positive or negative impact on the market. However, while other stocks recovered soon after, NBL remained around forty-naira per share for more than three years.

> The good trader watches profit taking
> opportunities carefully but runs like a
> deer at the first sign of adversity.

> Van Tharp

On the brighter side, I bought Con Oil shares at about thirty-five naira per share and sold them for more than one-hundred-and-twenty naira per share. However, the share price would climb to a high of one-hundred-and- seventy naira before sliding down to its present price of about sixty naira. At that time the Federal Government of Nigeria had just privatized National Oil which was purchased by a billionaire entrepreneur. With the change of name, injection of new funds into the company, improved performance, and the predictions of bonuses and high dividends, the price of the company's

shares now renamed Con Oil soared. I was a beneficiary of the combined effects of all these factors.

In the year 2007, I bought Fidelity Bank shares at about two naira and sold them for nine-naira-fifty- kobo per share. The share price would eventually go up to thirteen naira per share before it was put on technical suspension at eleven naira just before a public offer. I had come back from the Christmas and New Year celebrations with little cash left in my account As expected so my focus was on the penny stocks in response to the dictates of my pocket. While reviewing the stock page in the newspaper, my attention was drawn to Fidelity Bank stocks which were then selling for about two naira per share. I projected that being one of the successful banks in the consolidation process, the price of the stock had only one direction to move, and that is upwards. In between the two naira that I bought the shares initially and the nine naira at which I eventually sold them, I had sold and bought again several times as the price fluctuates mostly upwards.

I remember traveling to Onitsha, a town in eastern Nigeria to convince one of my best friends who was then the regional manager of a bank to invest in the stock market. After much talk, my friend reluctantly invested in NBL and First Bank shares. While he lost money in the NBL shares which he is quick to remind me of any time we discuss stock, he made a substantial amount of profit from the First Bank shares. I was glad when he told me recently that he had sold a portion of his holdings in First Bank shares to pay his brilliant daughter's school fees in Philadelphia, USA.

Sometimes, a lot of people under-utilize their resources due to lack of information. My friend who was then a branch manager of a bank in Nnewi; a commercial town in Anambra state south-east Nigeria was managing his family funds in a deposit account with a bank. The deposit at that time was yielding twelve percent interest per annum. After a lengthy discussion on the prospects of the stock market, he was

convinced of the huge potentials therein but did not have the capital to invest in the market. Based on the information, he gave to me, I advised him to move the funds from the deposit account to the subsidiary of my company where we would use the deposit as collateral to fund his initial investment in the stock market. At first, he was jittery and uncertain of his family's reaction to such a decision but after a week of persuasion, my friend took the decision to invest in the Nigerian Stock Market.

Fortunately, in less than six months, he had made over fifty percent returns on his investment. Today, he is a regional manager and controls a stock portfolio size of more than fifty-million naira. Each time we meet, he asks me what would have become of him if he had failed to take the decision then. Today he is a happy man even though his status car; a Honda Civic has not changed in the past eight years; evidence of the unfair treatment he has received from his employers over the years.

Another good friend of mine who had left her employment on matters of principle after the bank consolidation exercise is now an inspiration to the sit-tight Staff who love wearing their 'slave coats' every day to work and are afraid to leave their comfort zones and venture into the world they consider unknown. They are like the H&H in the book titled "Who Moved My Cheese" who are afraid of change. My friend has done exceedingly well in the stock market where she now has stock worth over a quarter-of-a-billion naira in her portfolio in less than one year. I recently asked her how she was doing; the response was breath-taking— 'I wish I had started earlier'. She now has more time to spend with her two lovely children and still makes more money annually than she did as a DGM [Deputy General Manager] in the bank. She is currently working on owning her own stock brokerage firm even if it is in conjunction with other people.

It is difficult to get a man to understand
something when his salary depends upon
his not understanding it.

Upton Beall Sinclair

As a CEO, during one of my trips to some of the West African Countries in pursuance of business development and relationship management, I came across a fine young man from my community who resides in Lome, the capital of the Republic of Togo. Although he is quite young, he is a highly respected international businessman held in high esteem by many who have had business dealings with him. In our discussions on international business and the adverse effects of the diminishing returns on investments [ROI] all over the world, I introduced investment in the Nigerian Stock Market as a viable investment option with high returns comparable to any in the World. At first, he was skeptical but was persuaded by the fact of my background and his trust in my reputation. He started with an initial investment of ten-million naira less than four years ago.

Today, he has a stock portfolio of more than two-hundred-and-fifty-million naira without bank facilities. Investment in stock has not only become a viable business option but also a dependable retirement plan for him. He calls me regularly from wherever he is in the world to follow- up on his stock investment.

The next friend of mine is a good example of the success of business portfolio diversification by our businessmen. My friend was a successful Foreign Exchange (FX) trader. He had dealt with some banks and major Bureau De Change operators and was known throughout the Lagos metropolis. However, with the liberalization of the foreign exchange market by the Central Bank of Nigeria, margins thinned out and his business was at risk with reduced patronage from traders and other clients who had access to FX from the Banks at competitive prices. It was at this point that I introduced him to the stock market. As CEO of a group of companies which included a stock brokerage firm, I was searching for new and reliable clients to convert to investors in the stock market and at the same time, boost my company's performance. Because my friend was very cautious, we started by investing only in blue chip companies which commanded our interest and confidence. With the passage of time and rapid capital appreciation, my friend started developing interest and more money was diverted from his regular business to the stock market.

Today, his major business is in the stock market with a total portfolio approaching one-billion naira. He obtained facilities in the range of two-hundred-and-fifty to five-hundred-million Naira from banks and stock brokerage firms to support his new trade in the stock market. I am delighted each time I see him, and we meet quite regularly. Interestingly, most of his colleagues in the FX trade are still counting their losses.

From the above illustrations, you can make lots of money in the stock market with proper advice, volume purchase, staying the course or cutting your losses short, having an articulated exit plan [without being unduly greedy] and access to relevant information, etc. However, always remember that there is a downside to it and that nobody can protect or grow your money more than you. Therefore, get involved and don't leave the decision to the Stockbroker alone.

People make money in the market by finding
themselves, achieving their potential, getting
in tune with the market...and a system or methodology
That is right for them

Van Tharp

The Nigerian Stock Market Crash.

The Nigerian stock exchange had grown steadily over a period of twenty years with very few noteworthy incidents. That was until well into the new millennium when a combination of internal and extraneous factors gave rise to an unprecedented boom in the sub sector. The share prices of several companies literally went through the roof, some of them doubled and the prices of some trebled within a space of a few months. This continued until the second quarter of 2008 when the crash came.

Some people attributed the Nigerian stock market crash to the current global recession. However, a review of the stock market would reveal that prices of stock in the Nigerian stock exchange were already nose-diving before the World economic meltdown. Therefore, market watchers concluded that the crash was a combination of factors including the following:

❖ The introduction of a policy by the Central Bank of Nigeria [CBN] restricting Commercial Banks from margin trading [giving loans to individuals or corporate entities to buy shares], though the Bank would later reverse its position.

❖ Companies that did not have strong fundamentals experienced an upward movement of their share prices by simply manipulating the laws of demand and supply [an artificial scarcity of the shares of those companies would be created and naturally when something is scarce the price goes up]. The bubble had to bust some time and it did in 2008.

❖ Foreign investors who had been attracted by the prospects of capital gains in the Nigerian stock market which was posting figures that were better than what they could get in their own countries withdrew their funds when the global recession became imminent.

Effective demand for shares went down and so did the prices.

It is pertinent however to state that regardless of the travails of the Nigerian stock market in the past few months, trading is going on in the stock exchange daily and as many people know; anytime buying and selling takes place, money is made and lost.

For example, I sold nearly three-hundred-thousand units of Access Bank shares about five weeks ago [April 2009] at four naira-eighty kobo per share. Whoever bought those shares would have more than doubled his investment if he decides to sell now [May 2009] because those shares are currently selling for nine-naira-eighty kobo. In this case, my loss was another person's gain.

In Summary, the stock market offers three distinct advantages among others as an investment option:

- Regular returns on investments through dividend payments which come at least once in a year for good stock.
- Share price appreciation or capital gains which have gotten as high as two hundred percent in less than a year.
- Bonus shares which are occasionally issued by companies to their shareholders in proportion to their existing shareholdings. You should also bear in mind that money invested in stock is almost immediately accessible. A shareholder can receive cash value for his shares within a maximum of seventy-two hours. The transaction date plus two days [T+2].

Understanding the Option (Stock) Trading:

I will conclude our discussion here with a short expository on Option Trading. Since my retirement, I have been engaged on a part-time basis in Option Trading.

What is an Option Contract in Stock Trading?

Option Contract gives the contract buyer the right but not the obligation to purchase and/or sell the underlying shares at a strike price. Every single contract covers 100 shares of the underlying stock.

Thus, Option contract gives the buyer leverage to access many more shares that wouldn't have been possible with the same level of funding.

How do you determine what and when to buy a share?
There are two types of analysis:

1. Fundamental Analysis. This analysis reviews the track record and performance of the company. It focuses on the company's earnings and net income which reflects the company's sales, growth, and debt valuation. So, the fundamental analysis will help you decide which company to buy. It's very useful for long term investors with the goal of growing their wealth in the stock market over a long period of time.

2. Technical Analysis. This analysis reviews the price trend of a particular share. The key focus here is the Uptrend (Bull) and the Downtrend (Bear). During the uptrend, the price makes a series of higher highs and higher lows, making the price tend upwards. If you project an upward trend in the price of a stock, you can buy a Call Option. On the other hand, in a Downward Trend, the price makes a series of lower highs and lower lows, making the

price trend downward. When you project this downward trend in price of stock, you can buy a Put Option.

There is also a price in Consolidation where the price is hitting the same highs and lows. Price in consolidation can either break out in a Downward or Upward trend.

In all three price trends above, you must look and wait for Confirmation i.e., a further price action to see the direction of the share before you make a trade entry.

The Technical analysis is most useful for short term Option Traders like the Day and Swing Traders.

What are some key terminologies you need to understand in share trading?

Going Short:
This means that the trader is selling high and buying low. This happens mostly in a Bearish market.

Going Long:
This means that the trader is buying low and selling high OR buy high and sell Higher. This usually happens in a Bull Market.

Ask price:
This represents the price that the seller is willing to sell the share.

Bid Price:
This represents the price that the buyer is willing to buy.

Spread:
The difference between the bid and the asking price.

Market order:
Ensures that you are in the trade. Sometimes, you might have to pay a premium to get in the order.

Limit Order:
Ensures that you enter the trade only if the market comes to your desired price. You may be able to enter the trade at a lower price. However, you might miss the move/trend as you want to trade against the momentum.

Stop Order (Buy):
Ensures that you enter the trade only if the market moves in your favor. You are entering the trade in a momentum. However, it might be a false breakout.

Stop Loss Order:
Enables you to exit the trade if the price goes against you. It helps cut your losses. But the market could reverse back in your direction. It's indeed a defense mechanism but not full proof.

Useful Tips in Option Trading:

>Never chase the market. If you miss a trend, wait for another opportunity.
>Never enter the market by guessing where the market is going.
>Never buy shares when the price is nearer to the Resistance level or sell at the Support level.
> Risk Management. Always limit the percentage of your trading fund that you want to risk on a particular share/trade at any time.

Investing In Real Estate

Buy land. They aren't making
any more of the stuff.

Will Rogers

Real estate is personal property in the form of buildings and land which can be used for residential, commercial of industrial purposes. To be financially independent, you must own your residential house. It's even better when the house can bring income into your pocket in the form of rent.

In the US, unlike in Nigeria, Mortgage is Key to owning a house and achieving one of the pillars of the American dream. To qualify for mortgage, the lenders will review your:

-Expense to Income Ratio; 25% to 45% recommended.

-Long term debt i.e., 10 months and above cannot be more than 36% of gross monthly Income

-Loan to Value Ratio.

-Above all, CREDIT HISTORY- borrowers with excellent credit history may be offered lower interest Rates. Review your credit history to confirm information therein before you apply.

Managing your credit entails that you stay within your limit, pay at least the Minimum due each month and when due and MINIMIZE your interest payment by Paying off the balance as quickly as possible. Finally, using less than 30% of your total approved credit limit enhances your credit rating.

The following will guide you in calculating your credit score:
- ~ Payment History/default 35%
- ~ How much you owe 30%
- ~ Length of credit history 15%
- ~ types and mix of credits 10%
- ~ New credit accounts and applications 10%.

So clearly, the longer your history of making timely payments, the higher your Credit score.

You will require the following documents from Lenders:
-Obtain a written pre-qualification.
-Loan disclosure/warranties.
-Rate lock in (rates can change between when you apply and closing)
-Processing Disclosure
-Transfer of loan servicing disclosure.
-The Appraisal-estimated value of your home.

Kinds/Characteristics of Mortgages:
-Fixed- where interest rates are fixed for the term of the loan.
-Variables- where interest rates usually start low and are adjusted periodically to reflect Inflation under advice to the borrower.
-Tenor could range from 5 years to 30 years. However, the shorter the tenor, the Less interest you pay on the loan.
-Down Payment refers to the cash you pay upfront. The more down payment amount You make, the less the monthly payment and vice versa.

Sources of Mortgage Loan:
-Retail banks, Credit Unions, Mortgage Bankers, and Insurance Companies.
-Federal Housing Adm. (FHA), Veterans Adm. (VA), State Programs to help the poor and first-time buyers.

The Mortgage Agreement: which must be read in detail contains the following information.
-Loan Amount
-Cost of the loan including Principal and   Interest charges.
-Repayment terms including tenor and periodic payments.
-Default clause and consequences.

Mortgage Advantages:

-Tax subsidies ranging in amounts depending on your tax brackets.

-Capital gains tax exclusion on a sale of primary home for at least 2 of the previous 5 years for the first $250,000.

-Auto savings otherwise known as Equity built up.

-Refinance option which allows you to take part of the equity to finance other Investments.

-Allows you to buy a house which otherwise you could not afford at the time of Purchase.

Mortgage Closing

-Before closing, the buyer should do the last inspection of the property and fund His/her account for the closing.

-Buyer should Respond to the Lender's request for further information usually to reconfirm the buyer's ratios before closing.

-On closing day, money is distributed to the lender, the seller and the Attorney and documents signed, and transfer of title effected.

-Remember that the major payments at closing are done with bank or cashier's Checks.

Finally, remember to consider the LOCATION and engage the services of professionals- real estate Agents or Attorneys as documentation relating to land must be in writing under the law.

With this background, let me tell you about my experience in Real Estate. The Richest Man in Babylon did not only teach me to save but also to invest in Real Estate. The book clearly restates the facts that to be financially independent, you must own your own house and if your house can bring money into your pocket in the form of rent, the better.

After reading the book, I decided to build my own house. The first thing I did was to envision the house I wanted to build in my mind. The house of my dreams was a five-bedroom single home with lots of green areas. But after I had sketched it and called an Architect to develop it, the cost was beyond my reach. So, I decided to build the house in two parts.

Firstly, I built a three-bedroom bungalow in 1994; and in 2001, I completed the second half of the house (a two bedroom) and merged it with the existing three bedroom. Today, I have my five-bedroom house with two living rooms and a garden. Amazingly, you cannot tell that the two houses were built separately and at different periods.

After envisioning my dream house in my mind, the next thing I did was to find the location. Location is very important in deciding where to build your house because that is the place you are likely to live for a long time. Moreover, location determines the value of the property over time. The decision in choosing a location is made more difficult if the area you have in mind is not yet developed at the time of taking the decision, so you have no guide in determining the future of the neighborhood.

I found a piece of land in the undeveloped part of the Government Residential Area [GRA] Ogudu, Lagos and paid two-hundred-and-fifty-thousand naira for it. This was in the middle of the June 12 crisis in 1993 when non- indigenes of Lagos state were packing their luggage and leaving for their home states in view of the political uncertainty in the region. The crisis was the fallout of the annulment of the Nigerian Presidential elections [held on the 12th of June] believed to have been won by international businessman, Chief M. K. O Abiola. My friends wondered why I took such a decision at that point in time. I wasn't certain then what prompted me. Perhaps it was gut feeling, but I did it and today, the price of a plot of land on Ina Obasi Street, now a major street in the Ogudu GRA Valley in Lagos is more than fifteen- million naira.

When you find the land, I advise that you engage the services of professionals like lawyers in the search and documentation of your title, an architect in the design, and an engineer in the construction of the house. Please do not cut corners here, because it could be disastrous. I have seen lots of money go down the drain at any of these stages of development. An improper foundation could result in a building that is unfit for human habitation and loss of substantial sums of money. Unfortunately, one of my neighbors is still battling with the problem of a faulty foundation several years after he had completed the building.

To be financially independent,
you must own your own property [house]

Richard Clawson

As the first staff in my Company to own a house of my own in Lagos, a lot of people looked up to me for advice on property development. I remember my friend [now an assistant general manager in a bank] who was having series of problems with his landlord. At that point in time, he had a plot of land in the Lekki-Ajah area of Lagos. With only six months to the end of the tenure of his existing lease, we started the process of building my friend his own house. He had an elaborate building plan which we reviewed together and decided to build it in phases. After decking the ground floor, he channeled all his effort into finishing and making it habitable. Thus, within six months, he was able to move into the ground floor of the house while he gradually completed the rest of the building. When he did the calculations, he found out that one year's rent in the luxurious duplex where he lived before embarking on the project was what he required to complete the first phase of his building project. He was so overwhelmed on the day he moved into his own house that he visited me with his family and brought along a bottle of Remy Martin in a show of appreciation for helping him say goodbye to "Landlord palaver".

In one of my holiday trips to the United States, I met one of the finest Nigerians living in California through a family friend. This man, from Edo State south-south Nigeria is a professional and an entrepreneur who owns and manages a courier company with branches all over Los Angeles and environs. Due to his interest in establishing a business back home, we spent a lot of time talking about investment opportunities in Nigeria each time we met. But his major constraint was finding a Nigerian who lived in Nigeria that he could trust.

During one of our discussions, he indicated interest in owning a house in a good location in Lagos, south- west Nigeria. I promised to assist him locate a suitable property when I got back to Nigeria. Back in Nigeria, I went to visit a friend in Crown Estate along the Lekki Peninsular. Once in the estate, I knew it was the exact kind of place my friend was looking for. I enquired about the cost of acquiring property there and got details which were relayed to my friend. He was excited. Within one month and without even seeing the property, he paid for it. As a lawyer experienced in the requirements for building design and construction, I ensured that the documentation was concluded without delay.

The next stage was to build the house of his dreams. My friend had sent across a building plan which we [a team comprising of an Engineer, an Architect, and my humble self-] had amended to suit the realities on ground. We got the necessary approvals from the local government authorities and soon were ready to commence construction. It was at this point that my friend visited Nigeria

Because I did not have the time for daily supervision of the project, I engaged the services of a trustworthy building engineer. The construction of the house was broken up into stages with measurable milestones. Funds were released in strict compliance to the successful execution of each milestone. Now the house is almost completed requiring only minor finishing touches; incidentally my friend did not visit Nigeria throughout the period of construction. However, photo updates from the Engineer were sent to him regularly to keep him abreast of progress made at every stage. In recent tele- phone discussions, I have stressed the need for him to visit home at this crucial finishing stage to enable him to make personal input in the choice of items to be used.

To his amazement, all through the period of construction, we exhibited professionalism in our work thereby engendering his trust. Funds sent to me were judiciously applied to the project and proper accounts rendered. As the project comes to an end, we have succeeded in allaying his fears about doing business in Nigeria and with Nigerians. His candid opinion is that I am a wonderful person and a rare breed of Nigerian.

On my part I am delighted to have made him regain trust and confidence in his countrymen by helping him acquire a magnificent house in the lovely, serene environment of Crown Estate.

> Financial sense is knowing that
> certain men will promise to do
> certain things and fail.
>
> Ed Howe

When I first got to the subsidiaries as CEO, I met this focused young man who had just begun his career in the insurance arm of the subsidiary. Over time, I noticed that this young man was troubled. One day, I called him into my office and enquired what his problem was. Initially, he was reluctant to open to me because the issue had to do with his unit-head.

Eventually he did and narrated how he was being threatened and frustrated by his supervisor for reasons unknown to him. Being a supervisor to his supervisor, I understood his plight. His supervisor is a believer in the old school of management where the boss is all- knowing and ruthless. I had confronted her on a few occasions about her management style which I considered over- bearing and counterproductive.

I was touched by his agonizing stories of frustrations leading to his abrupt decision to quit the job. I decided to intervene in his plight by giving him lessons on financial independence. I started by reminding him that as an employee in a financial institution, he was among the top ten percent of highly paid Nigerians.

Consequently, his happiness and future success were in his hands. With proper focus and set goals, he could become whatever he wanted to be in life. I told him the story of another young man who had come to me 'red eyed' when his supervisor had recommended him to be transferred from Lagos to Onitsha. I told the young man then that the reason for his tears could be traced to financial insecurity. Otherwise, he would have summoned up courage to explain to his supervisor why he could not leave Lagos at that material time due to cogent family reasons.

Certainly, most employees tolerate a lot of injustice and abuse in the hands of their bosses due to job and financial insecurity. Therefore, if you want to rule your world, you must begin early to plan for your future. You must make the necessary sacrifice, save, and invest in assets that would instill confidence in you to face the World and challenge the status quo when necessary. The earlier you start the better.

The young man understood my illustrations and was propelled to take action that day concerning his future. With my encouragement, he bought two plots of land in Ikorodu, a suburb of Lagos; and with his up-front payment fenced the land and commenced construction of a four-bedroom bungalow. I approved his application for a soft loan when he got to the roofing stage. Today, the young man who is at the third level in the subsidiary [an equivalent of an assistant bank officer] is a proud owner of his own house. He is no longer a pawn in the hands of his boss and the sky is his limit.

A lot of people make the mistake of waiting to get all the money required to build a house before they start. So, they never get to start. When I was building my three-bedroom house, there were times all the cash I had in my bank account was less than five-thousand naira. But the urge to continue was overwhelming because I was seeing the evidence of every naira I invested in the house. That gave me a lot of fulfillments. Once you start, you won't want to stop until the house is completed.

By June 1994, I was already living in my own house. This gave me a lot of savings since I did not have to pay rent and the confidence to face the World without having any undue pressure to make money in an unprofessional manner. Since then, I have built other houses for commercial purposes with the help of mortgage loans from the banks and income from my investments in stocks. Remember, if you must invest in commercial property, you must learn how to deal with tenants.

Unlike most other investments, Real Estate has the best chances of multiplying in value over time. Thus, it tends to be the most reliable and stable of all the investment options. This is the reason why some investors reinvest income earned from the stock market in Real Estate. However, the 2008 real estate collapse in the US [which I believe is temporary] is food for thought. A lot of people get into trouble with mortgage finances due to their lack of understanding of the terms and conditions of the mortgage. I once took a mortgage facility from a bank. After paying the monthly installments for one year totaling over two-million naira, I realized that less than three-hundred-thousand naira out the total repayments I had made had gone to the repayment of the principal sum. The balance of over one- million-seven-hundred-thousand naira went to interest payments only. This is so because of the high interest charges on mortgages by banks in Nigeria. To minimize my cost, I was compelled to source for funds to repay a substantial portion of the principal and restructure the outstanding balance for a shorter tenor thereby denying me the main advantage of a mortgage. If I had continued with the previous arrangement, I would have had to pay the principal sum four times by the end of the fifteen- year tenor. That is twice what a normal mortgage would have cost me.

I once had a discussion with my brother [a Chartered Public Accountant in the United States] on the issue of mortgages in the US during which we reviewed the current state of the US mortgage sub sector and the adverse effect on millions of house owners, we concluded that for effective use of mortgage as a finance option, one would need the services of an expert who will explain in detail the implications of the terms and conditions of the mortgage. Most mortgagors have lost their houses because they lack understanding of the stipulations of the mortgage, especially as it relates to the repayment of principal and interest. The situation is worse for people with low credit ratings in the US while unstable cash flow and high interest charges cripple many people in Nigeria.

A fool and his money are soon parted.

anonymous

Investment In Your Own Business.

I am successful because I have always been a tortoise.
I do not come from a rich family.
I did not finish school.
I am not particularly talented. Yet, I am far richer than
most people, simply because I did not stop.

Robert Kiyosaki

Investing in your own business is one of the most challenging and at the same time, the most rewarding of the investment options. This so because, 50% businesses fail within the first five years of their existence. Therefore, to own your own business, you must consider the following:

-Seek support of your family because of its impact on them and you.

-Seek support of professional advisors- Attorney, Accountant, Banker etc.in choosing the type of business and its funding.

-You must research on the business, type, location, name availability, business permit etc.

-Review the funding options. If you need to partly fund the business by borrowing from the bank, you need to order, review your credit report, and determine your credit worthiness.

-Find a gap in the market to be filled and fill it with service at the appropriate price.

-Know what competition is doing and evaluate them.

-Do your business plan, cost, and projections.

-Always be guide by the principle that if you cannot grow your business, you must cut cost and reinvest you Profit.

-Know how to reach and delight your customers as they are key to the success of your business. The following will help:

Acknowledge customers by name in all communication.

Keep relationship with customers simple e.g. handwritten thank you letters go a long way.

Create a customer service culture (CSC), document CSC expectation, track customer service performance, recognize, reward, and sanction employees accordingly.

Stay close to customers after sales using internet, follow up, and resolve issues speedily.

-Use technology to enhance your efficiency in the following areas not withstanding its cost:

Financial management software helps track sales, expenses, receivables, monitor Inventory purchases, pay roll, cash flow management, etc.

Customer relationship management (CRM) software helps in providing customer data, minimize sales, minimizing costs, and helps customer retention.

-Use online and mobile banking to manage and monitor your account 24/7.

-Use website and online marketing to create awareness of your products, create and engage customers.

-Apply cloud computing for information storage and to facilitate file sharing etc.

-Above all, grow your PASSION in the business as passion is the key to driving your business.

I do not have a lot of personal experience in managing certain types of businesses since most of my business experience resolved around managing financial/professional related institutions like Finance House, Stockbrokerage, Insurance and Law Firms. So, I decided to illustrate this topic of owning your business with the experiences of my own Abiriba Entrepreneurs. They are reputed for their enterprising nature even prior to the era of government-induced entrepreneurs in Nigeria. I believe that you will learn a lot from their experiences, strengths, and weaknesses in managing their businesses. The next few paragraphs would review a few of the business successes of this enterprising people.

MY PEOPLE

(The Abiriba Experience)

God gave me my money. I believe the power
to make money is a gift from God to be developed
and used to the best of our ability for the goodof
mankind. Having been endowed with the gift
I possess. I believe it is my duty to make money
and still make more money and to use the money
I make for the good of my fellow man according to
the dictates of my conscience.

John D. Rockefeller

I come from the ancient Town of Abiriba known by many as
'Small London'. The sobriquet small London came from the
right honorable Dr. Nnamdi Azikiwe, the first president of
Nigeria; this was because way back in the days before Nigeria
attained independence the town had electricity, a good network
of roads, schools, hospitals, pipe-borne water, and some of the
most magnificent edifices in that part of the country. A replica
of the famous Big Ben in London is one of the interesting
monuments in the town.

From time immemorial, my people have been famous
entrepreneurs known for their shrewdness in managing their
own businesses. They are daring, engaging in businesses that
many would not dare to. They made lots of money from trading
and became famous throughout Igbo land [the Igbo people
of south-east Nigeria are known all over the world for their
business acumen and enterprising nature]. Our indigenous
words like 'kaa' and 'okpogho' became generally accepted and
used in the commercial city of Aba, south-east Nigeria, and
some other West African Countries where they were doing

business. With their Age-Grade System, they provided the basic infrastructures that made the community a star among its neighbors and a shining example of a community in our great country Nigeria, built largely through self-effort.

The Abiriba indigenous system of governance was unique in the sense that it operated as a monarchy which also had a developed democratic system in place.

o The Enachioken-in-council comprising the Ukpaghari of Amaogudu, Abiriba, the Efa of Agboji, Abiriba, the Enachioken of Abiriba, and the Ikwukwuma perform both the executive and the legislative functions of the community.

o The age-grade system which consists of thirteen age-grades is key to the Abiriba culture and its development. The age-grades were formed by placing members of the community in groups according to their year of birth-three years apart. Each age-grade at its own turn is charged with taking care of the social and infrastructural development of the town. They do this by taxing themselves, imposing levies or applying what- ever means they deemed necessary to achieve their objective. When an age-grade had served the community for upwards of forty years; members of that age-grade proceed on retirement and are hosted by the community in a ceremony known as "Uche" where family, friends and the entire members of the community are expected to give precious gifts to the retirees for their service to the community.

o The Uke Ji Agbala and the Uke Igwa Mang were charged with leading in administration, enforcing the laws made by the Enachioken-in-council, securing, and defending the community against any external aggression.

o The Inyimoka and Umon act as the chambers of commerce; promoting trade, ensuring that trade secrets were kept, and settling trade disputes among the indigens of Abiriba in their business locations within and outside the community. They also had the power to sanction erring members.

With this sophisticated system of government that has been in place for over one-hundred years, my people were able to build an egalitarian society more advanced than its contemporaries in any other part of the country. This enabled them to provide basic infrastructure and social amenities like the general hospital in Abiriba; arguably the largest in that part of the country when it was built and commissioned in 1960 by Akahaba [my late father's age-grade]. The hospital was consequently named Akahaba General Hospital after the age-grade. Sir Akanu Ibiam; an executive member of the World Council of Churches and a former governor of the defunct Eastern Region of Nigeria was the Chief Medical Director of this reputable institution for many years.

Another project built entirely by communal effort is Enuda College built in 1954, during the years of British colonial rule. Government policy at that time required an approval from the District Commissioner [DC] before the school could be built. The District Commissioner was a Briton who was resident in Umuahia, the district headquarters at the time. After the preambles the DC asked the community for representatives who would stand as guarantors ensuring their financial capacity to build the school. At this juncture "the big five"- the five most prominent citizens of Abiriba community drove from Port-Harcourt and Calabar [from where they administered their business empires] to Umuahia in five Limousines, one of which was a Pontiac. When the DC saw the five luxury cars pull up in front of his office, he did not hesitate to sign the approval documents for the school. That was 1954; whoever could afford five luxury cars including a Chevrolet and a Pontiac in Sub Saharan Africa could have no problem financing the construction of a secondary school. The exalted DC himself was the proud owner of a bicycle.

However, in the past decade, as the business environment changed, many of them were unable to change along with the times due mainly to ignorance. Consequently, the wealth that was accumulated up to the mid-1990s has been substantially diminished.

Today, some of my people who had thriving businesses and owned lots of buildings in the commercial city of Aba are now jobless and living in rented apartments having sold their houses just to reinvest the money in the same businesses that are no longer profitable. It still baffles me how a businessman who made lots of money from a line of business and built several houses could stay in the same business and lose everything without knowing when to stop and move on. This is more so as government policies were becoming very unfavorable to the business. In most cases the reinvested funds simply went down the drain. My people continued without realizing that they could have simply remained Landlords or property owners, leveraging on the ever-increasing property appreciation, and collecting whatever revenue accruing to them as rent from their properties.

What happened? Substantially, ignorance and lack of knowledge of changing business environment, skills, and changing Government policies are largely responsible. Many of my people stuck to their lines of business ignorant of the changing business world. As major importers, they were unable to come together to challenge the monopolistic tendencies posed by the middlemen (Distributors) who started to undercut them in pricing when they lost a major portion of their working capital arising from government seizures.

Some invested wrongly in non-income yielding assets such as magnificent country homes where they barely spend two weeks in a whole year and by so doing tied down their working capital. A few were out rightly extravagant, living well above their incomes. Others were over-leveraged and got smothered by the high cost of funds and bank charges. Some others just refused to move on to other businesses or to reinvest and diversify their investment portfolios.

But the few that kept faith with the rules and ethics of business, constantly renewing their skills, having passion for what they were doing, associating pain/night- mares with failure, diversified their portfolios by investing in Stocks, Real Estate, and other new lines of growing businesses such as Banking, Telecommunications, Oil and Gas, etc., survived. Thus, they expanded their horizons and continued to contribute towards making Abiriba the "Small London" as it used to be known. Below are some examples of a few who were able to expand and diversified their businesses in line with the current changes in the economy.

Prior to 1980, the businesses of my people were predominantly importation of textiles. However, this great son of Abiriba was a giant in the importation of stock fish and was a renowned leader in the business worldwide. He was a prominent politician in his time and was conferred with the award of Officer of the Federal Republic OFR by the Federal Government of Nigeria for his political and economic achievements.

Towards the end of his business career, he decided to diversify into manufacturing. He built a paper mill with a converter along the banks of the Imo River in Abia state south-east Nigeria. His products which consisted mainly of tissue paper instantly became a household name. In less than five years, he broke away from the traditional business of importation of finished goods associated with my people.

When he passed on, the mantle of leadership of the fledgling business fell on his son who is an exposed, shrewd, and deep-thinking young man with a master's degree. The burden on him from the business and within the family was enormous. Despite the challenges he faced, the young Chairman/CEO marched on, exhibiting a high sense of maturity in his business decisions. He started by expanding the industrial base of the factory. He then skillfully negotiated and purchased adjourning lands to the factory in anticipation of future expansion and development. Thereafter, he proceeded to import brand new high-tech equipment to support his planned expansion into the second phase.

After successfully modernizing the factory, he embarked on new lines of products like sanitary ware, stationeries, and a printing press. He also improved on the quality of the existing product, tissue paper. Despite the enormous economic and policy challenges facing the manufacturing sector in Nigeria, this CEO along with his executive management team comprising mostly of his siblings have successfully built a modern Conglomerate-one of the best in its sector in the country. Unfortunately, the organization suffered tremendous set back in the middle of the 2000s and did not recover thereafter.

Another pillar of our community is a middle-aged man. He started his business career quite early and had been involved in all lines of our people's traditional businesses. He is loved by many and hated by others for his outspoken nature and domineering presence. A flamboyant person by disposition; this man built one of the most magnificent country homes in our community. In the mid-1990s, he diversified into telecommunications. As a pioneer operator, a lot of people were surprised at the level of success he attained within a short while. He commenced the telecommunications operations from the Enyimba city of Aba which was his operational base and within a short time; he had expanded the coverage of his company throughout the south-east; from Eket in Akwa Ibom state to Onitsha in Anambra state through the length and breadth of Cross River, Imo, Rivers, and Abia states. His continuous reinvestment in the business and improved personalized service delivery endeared him to his numerous customers including the giant multinationals like Mobil in Eket where he was their sole service provider as at that time.

With the liberalization of the telecommunications sector in 2001, his company became the telecoms company of choice in the Eastern part of Nigeria. The liberalization also brought with it foreign investors with experience, capital, and modern technology with the attendant increase in competition. Many of the new companies approached him for business cooperation, mergers, or buy-outs. Like a shrewd businessman, he weighed his options, did his calculations, and opted to sell. The sale price which ran into several billions of Naira was unprecedented in that part of the country. With the funds realized from the sale, he could start off and nurture any business of his choice and still live like a king in any part of the World. I admire his foresight in building such a reputable first-class company and his willingness to sell same. Most people would have clung to the ownership of the company to their own detriment.

The next pillar of our community has a different background than the others. From inception the two brothers agreed not to engage in the importation of textiles which was the flag ship product of my peoples' line of business. Immediately after the Nigerian civil war, they concluded that there would be a need for massive reconstruction in south-eastern Nigeria ravaged by the devastating Nigerian-Biafra War [1967- 1970]. So, the duo decided to engage in the business of building materials. Their major product was cement even though they also dealt in Steel products, rice, etc.

According to their business plan, the younger brother would relocate to Port Harcourt to take advantage of the seaport facilities and establish contact with international suppliers while the older brother would remain in Aba managing and investing the proceeds of the business. Every weekend, the two would meet in Aba to review progress reports and strategize on the way forward. This process continued for over a decade.

In the process of time, the bond between the two brothers grew and their business flourished. It was like a miracle- two individuals with one mind. The love and unity they shared transcended to their children to the extent that it is difficult today to distinguish between the older brother's children and his younger brother's because they all act like they are from the same parents. They are a glowing example of love and unity of purpose shared between two brothers; a feat many have tried to accomplish without success.

With the proceeds from their business, the two brothers ventured into Real Estate: specializing in the development of industrial estates. They built massive commercial and industrial warehouses all over the Umungasi area of Aba and acquired vast portions of land in Port Harcourt and its environs. However, with the devaluation of the Naira in the mid-1980s, the funds required to import a shipload of cement became astronomical. They were compelled by circumstances to diversify. In partnership with their Italian friends, they incorporated an oil services company. Today, the multi-million-dollar oil services company is a giant in engineering and marine construction in the oil -rich Niger Delta region. They further embarked on the production of bottled water in one of the industrial estates in Aba and started by installing state-of-the –art equipment and created business environment unrivalled by the competition. Their bottled water soon became the best within their target market. The personalized labeling of their bottles to suit various occasions has made their product the toast of their distributors and the delight of their customers. My siblings and I are beneficiaries of the love, unity and achievements shared by these two brothers. The amazing reality is that after the passing of the two brothers, their children have continued to manage the various family business organizations. They have shown that with love, you can conquer anything as they are to a large extent, the only family of its peers in Abiriba still surviving in unity and making progress a family.

Another pillar is a dynamic young man. From his early years, he was unusually endowed with abundant commonsense and natural skills. He came from a very comfortable background as his father was among the 'Big Five' in my community in the middle of the twentieth century. He started his business life under the watchful eyes of his Nna-ukwu [Master or a mentor] who was then a major player in general commerce in the city of Aba.

Expectedly, he continued in this line of business when he disengaged from his master and started his own business. However, his eyes were set on something higher. In one of his trips to the United States in the early nine - ties, he met one of the leading cosmetic companies in the World. In the negotiations that ensued between his company and the international cosmetics conglomerate, the young man exhibited his business skills to the admiration of his would-be partners. He started off as a distributor of their beauty care products in Nigeria and ended up with a franchise for West Africa. Unlike most of his colleagues who had acquired distributorship contracts with other large international conglomerates, his relationship with this foreign company blossomed in the face of the massive increase in sales volumes of the company's products all over West Africa.

Earlier in the relationship, he had realized the need for market dominance in his target market. He there- fore decided to relocate his business from Aba to Lagos; a decision that would eventually take him to the top. Today, he is one of the most successful young men in my community. He is a master planner and skillful negotiator endowed with a pleasant character and an amiable personality. He is an acclaimed leader in the franchise business. His country home is a lovely sight; an architectural masterpiece crafted by one who is a master in his own field, and which significantly portrays his sterling qualities.

This beautiful edifice set in a serene environment will remain one of the most beautiful monuments in our community for years to come. Today, the wife along with her children are successfully managing the Business empire this exceptional Pillar of our community left behind.

The next pillar is an industrialist-investor. He realized early in his business life that Lagos is the business capital of Nigeria and decided to play there. Although his business had branches in Aba and other parts of the country, his head office was in Lagos where he resides. He started from our traditional importation of finished goods and became very successful in products like tiles, carpets, rugs, rubberized textiles etc. [I bought the floor tiles for my house in Lagos from his company in 1994]. From importation to manufacturing, he distinguished himself in business circles within the Lagos metropolis and beyond. Over a period, he built an industrial estate in the Lagos main land area where most of these products are manufactured.

In the late 1980s, he further diversified his line of business by making substantial investments in the stock market with emphasis in the banking sector. Unlike most of his contemporaries, he consistently maintained his hold in the companies he invested in. His early start in stock market investments aided him greatly in mastering the rules of the market which culminated in outstanding achievements for him. Today, his son sits on the board of directors of one of the most capitalized banks in Nigeria. From his luxurious mansion overlooking the lagoon in the Lekki peninsular area of Lagos, this shrewd, tough business mogul is in firm control of his various business ventures throughout Nigeria and beyond. Now, in retirement, he spends most of his time now with the family and grandchildren in the United States as he is no longer in charge of the day-to-day management his business empire.

Another pillar in our community is a young entrepreneur and industrialist. He started business quite early in life and went into the importation of textiles from Europe, the United

States and Asia. He was very successful in this business and became a known name in the textile market in Aba south-east Nigeria.

However, this young man's line of business would change drastically after the 1996 seizure of a shipload of containers carrying textile materials worth over one billion Naira belonging to importers from Aba at the Calabar ports. This singular act by the Nigerian Customs dealt a devastating blow to the Abiriba business community and would lead to communal crisis and destruction of property in the ancient town in subsequent years.

For this young entrepreneur, he saw this seizure as an opportunity to move on and diversify his lines of business. He started with a modern, well equipped photo processing laboratory on the ground floor of his head office building in Aba. He later brought in state-of-the- art equipment, provided an enabling infrastructure, employed, and trained personnel to effectively manage the operations of the photo lab. In less than six months, this Lab became the number-one film processing center in Aba. Encouraged by the success of the Aba office, this entrepreneur proceeded to replicate the photo processing centers throughout the major cities and towns in the south-east and south-south regions of Nigeria.

From film processing, he went into manufacturing and proceeded to build a multi-million-Naira vegetable oil processing plant in the Ogbor Hill area of Aba metropolis. Gradually, this entrepreneur has become a giant in this subsector inundating the market with new products from his modern plant.

Amazingly, he achieved all these despite the mounting adversity faced by the manufacturing sector in Nigeria due to inadequate infrastructure and bank financing. He succeeded by resorting to a massive reinvestment of profits from his previous and existing businesses. This unassuming, simple, and reserved young entrepreneur has thus, carved out a bright future for himself and his numerous businesses. With the increased insecurity in Nigeria, this successful entrepreneur had to relocate to the United States with his family from where he still manages his businesses from his comfort secure home.

The last of the pillars of our community is a brilliant example of the Abiriba entrepreneurial spirit. He started his career as a businessman at a very young age specializing in the Abiriba traditional lines of business. It did not take him long to manifest his business skills as he soon became a prominent figure in the business circles, dominating major areas of general commerce in the bustling city of Aba. As a young multi-millionaire, his dreams took him beyond commerce, and he diversified into manufacturing. He built one of the first family-owned breweries in that part of the country whose prime product competed favorably with the best in the industry. His brand was widely accepted and dominated the market in the old Imo and Cross River states particularly. Despite his resounding success with the brewery, he refused to rest on his oars and went on to build a paper factory which produced tissue paper and ancillary paper products.

From commerce to manufacturing, his story was one of unparalleled success. So, it was not a surprise to many when he ventured into another area previously unknown to our people. With the liberalization of the banking industry in the late 1980s, this illustrious son of Abiriba became one of the first individuals in the country to own majority equity in several banks. Consequently, he became a dominant figure in the banking industry in Nigeria prior to the mid-1990s. As Chairman of one of the leading banks in the country, he spearheaded the introduction of the now famous on- line real-time technology which revolutionized service delivery and endeared customers to the bank. The bank soon became an industry leader in the field of technology and relationship management by giving all stakeholders the right to succeed.

When he retired from active business, he continued to enjoy the fruits of his labor, oversee his vast business empire, and manage his enormous wealth created through hard work. For years to come, this business mogul, industrialist and entrepreneur par excellence will remain one of the best business minds ever produced by the Abiriba community, and an inspiration to the younger generation. Unfortunately, this huge empire of wealth is gradually being destroyed by family squabbles after the demise of the founder.

Finally, I have used these pillars of our ancient community to illustrate entrepreneurship and the power of business diversification in line with changing trends in the key areas of our economy namely, commerce, manufacturing, telecommunications, oil and gas and banking. I believe you would have been inspired as you read through their achievements and have learnt some- thing that would aid you in managing your business. Time and space constraints prevent me from telling you about several other people who have excelled in business and other areas of specialization such as the Academia, Medicine, the Military, Law and other areas of discipline, whose contributions to the development of our community have brought fame and improved the living standards of our people.

THE FAMILY

No man is an island. We all need relationships. Close
relationships built on faith create trust, leads to peace of mind
and abundant happiness; make the good times better and the
difficult times easier. A joy shared is a joy doubled,
but a problem shared is a problem halved.

Adam A. Jackson

While I was writing this book, my first son reminded me of
the role of the family in the investment plan. Thinking through
his suggestion, it was very clear to me that a supportive family
is essential in the successful execution of our investment plans.

For a married couple, the support of the spouse is a
major factor. A lot of families fail in the pursuit of financial
independence because the couples have divergent goals. While
one spouse may be inclined to live by the day, the other may be
propelled to save and invest for the rainy days.

For the spouses that live by the day, they are attracted by
the present. They want to buy the latest clothes and jewelry,
drive the latest models of cars, and live in expensive homes etc.,
even if they cannot afford such luxuries. They are interested
in what friends and neighbors say about them. They live their
tomorrow, today and their expenditure is more than their
earnings. For such people their happiest moments are when
they are spending money they have not earned. They are the
people that will max out their credit cards with the attendant
negative impact on their credit scores.

On the other hand, the spouses who want to save
and invest for the future are more concerned about living
comfortably for the rest of their lives. To do this, they believe
in investing in assets today, that would earn income to support
their expenditure tomorrow. They are less bothered by what
people say about them. They have their plans, set their goals

and consistent work to achieving the set goals. They will carry out their plans irrespective of what people say. Their happiest moment is when they achieve their set goals aimed at a better tomorrow.

When both spouses fall within the latter category, attaining financial independence is guaranteed in the family. This is made further easier when both spouses agree on various roles to play in their home. This agreement is vital as most homes have had major challenges due to the inability of the spouses to agree and accept certain roles. For example, it has been observed that where both spouses are engaged in very demanding jobs [that require them to leave very early in the morning and return home late at night], the home front suffers. This situation does not create a good atmosphere for investment decision-making. In such a situation, it may be beneficial to the family if one spouse looks for some- thing that would allow them more flexibility to manage their home effectively. In my own case I have been blessed with a family that believes in teamwork, understanding, love, and unity. I give my dear wife a lot of credit in this respect.

Before concluding this book, I would like to share with you all a bonus paper I presented titled:

Seven Habits That Inhibits Achievement of Financial Growth.

Many people go through life financially hindered because of their inability to understand their finances. As a results, they suffer various consequences with adverse implications on themselves and their loved ones.

This is the reason we set out to share with YOU, our knowledge and experience spanning over a period of 21 years in various management positions held in the Financial Sector. This ultimately culminated in the publishing of my award-winning book, Financial Independence, our main resource material.

Our enduring goal is to educate our readers on the knowledge needed to financially liberate oneself and how it can be implemented in their daily lives. One way we are doing this is by reviewing some of the habits that inhibits people from achieving financial independence and recommend alternative habits in what we refer to as "Good" and "Bad" Habits. We believe that a consistent application of these Good Habits will help you start a process of moving towards achieving your financial goal.

THE FIRST BAD HABIT: NOT SETTING GOAL.

Everyone dreams, but it's only those who take consistent steps to actualize their dreams that get to live the dream. Setting a goal is the first step in turning your dream to a reality.

You must understand why you are setting the goal and what is required to achieve the goal. To effectively do this, you must be sincere to yourself and evaluate your strengths and weaknesses, starting from your base and seek out ways to improve on your weaknesses.

Passion is the key that drive the process. The more passionate you are in setting and pursuing the goal, the better chances you have to achieving it. You can start by constantly envisioning what it will be like to achieve your set goal.

It is recommended that the goal be shared with your loved ones for effective buy in and support, be in writing, specific, measurable, and challenging. Challenging goals improve productivity and induce a high-performance culture that help you to achieve success.

Finally, without setting a goal, it's very difficult to achieve success. But just setting the goal is not enough, you must take Immediate and Consistent action to achieve the goal. To illustrate how important setting goal is, in an old Harvard study, college students that set goals just before their graduation achieved 10 TIMES MORE than their counterparts that did not, in ten years after graduation.

Therefore, Decide Today to write down your goal in detail, share it with your loved ones for their support in helping you achieve it, and take immediate and specific actions to actualize your set goal.

THE THIRD BAD HABIT: YOUR BELIEF IN NOT MAKING ENOUGH MONEY TO SAVE.

This erroneous belief was aptly debunked earlier in this book with the story of the Bank Branch Driver who thought he wasn't making enough money to start saving until his direct supervisor urged him to open a savings account and encouraged him to save 10% of his salary every month. The driver was amazed at his achievement after few years of consistent application of saving 10% of his salary. He was able to save enough to rent a three-bedroom flat and send his children to private school. The driver achieved this huge success with no increment in his salary and with no significant change in his lifestyle during the period.

Savings is simply generated when you live below your earnings. It entails distinguishing between your "needs" and "wants" and making sacrifices today for future security and perhaps, enjoyment.

Nobody can become financially independent without learning the habit of savings. That is why Financial Independence is like a three-legged stool resting on savings, insurance, and investment.

If you do not learn to save when your earning is small, it will certainly be difficult to save when your income increases. The reason is simple, the act of saving is a learned lifestyle/habit and not one that is dependent on how much money you make. That is why you see so many lottery winners reverting to status quo few years after winning the lottery.

Therefore, if you want to be Financially independent, decide today to pay yourself FIRST when you receive your next paycheck by putting 10% of it into your savings account. You will be amazed that nothing much will change in your

THE FOURTH BAD HABIT: FAILURE TO BUDGET.

A budget is simply a plan on how to spend your money with the aim of balancing your expenses with your income. The reason you do it in advance is to help you distinguish your "Needs" from your "Wants". The Word "Need" is defined in the dictionary as "requiring (something) because it is essential or very important" while "Want" is to "have a desire to possess or do (something); wish for". In other words, "Need" is what is essential for your survival as against "Want" which is not.

Quite often, many people never develop the habit of budgeting, and they end up spending all their income without a plan and sometimes before the income is even earned. If you are struggling with your finances, proper budgeting is a must for you. Your goal will be to cut off all the items on your "wants" list and review your " Needs" list to see how to prioritize the items therein and save even more.

You could start by implementing any of the following:

Putting off your annual family vacations.

Limiting your indulgence in some vices like smoking and alcohol consumption or clubbing. Buying a used car (recommends 3-year-old models with its added depreciation benefits) instead of a brand-new car. Avoid moving into a bigger house after you have substantially paid down your current mortgage. Patronizing thrift and other low-cost stores, the list goes on.

Alternatively, you can try budgeting by listing all your Assets (things that bring money to you) and your Liabilities (things that take money away from you) and determine how to increase your assets and reduce your liabilities. Thereafter, from your list of liabilities, determine which ones are your "Needs" and which ones are your "Wants" and prioritize ONLY to focus on your "Needs" going forward.

Whichever option you may chose, the idea is to free funds from your current expenditure pattern to enable you save more, pay off your debt and invest for your financial independence.

THE FIFTH BAD HABIT: THE TENDENCY TO OVERSPEND.

This Habit is closely related to the fourth bad habit of not budgeting. It causes people to spend more than they earn to compete with other people including friends, family members, neighbors, colleagues etc.

This is an ego trip habit that makes people want to do things to create an impression to outsiders knowing very well that they could not afford the lifestyle that they are pretending to live.

As teenagers, our father had told us in one of our regular discussion sessions (a unique feature of our family) with him, not to live a "false life". Curiously, I had asked him what he meant by false life? He replied with an idiomatic expression - "cut your cloth according to your size". Realizing that I was still a bit confused with his answer, he explained further that living a false life is when you spend more money than you earn. It's like living a life of false pretense which always only end up in ruins. That stuck in my brain ever since and helped lay a foundation for my simple lifestyle.

One way to avoid or minimize this bad habit of overspending is to be real to yourself and try to live within your means. For example, an elderly family (Husband and wife) with a reduced income and grown children out of the house, decided to sell one of their two cars and jointly use one car instead. This was possible because of their limited and compatible job schedules as each worked less than 30 hours every week. The couple's decision saved them over $500 in monthly car payments, insurance, taxes, and maintenance which they now reinvest in their retirement plan.

Other people have done this by budgeting and strictly following their budget stipulations. Some are taking advantage of the numerous opportunities abound in shopping for value where they utilize the huge savings offered by some discount outfits like GoodRX for prescription drug purchases which are free.

For shoppers, you will be amazed how much you will be saving by including coupons in your daily shopping. Simply goggle coupon and get a whole list of free coupon sources online.

So, decide Today NOT to live a false life by critically reviewing your expenditure pattern, always striving to live within your means and eliminate all liability expenditures more than your income. Live your life remembering that you are created uniquely by the Almighty God and need not stress yourself to be like others.

THE SIXTH BAD HABIT: THE UNWILLINGNESS TO STEP OUT OF ONE'S COMFORT ZONE.

"Stepping out of your comfort zone involves uncertainty and risk. However, most people shy away from taking risk and are afraid of venturing outside their comfort zone. They forget that whenever progress is made in any field of human endeavor, it had been accompanied by change. Changes comes with uncertainty and risk. If you fear taking risks, you will most likely remain the same and end up not achieving much financially in life. Remember, No Risk No Income". The above quotation was taken from my award-winning book titled Financial Independence.

Decide Today to do something different from your routine that is aimed at helping you achieve your financial independence. For example, a neighbor who lost his job due to the Covid-19 Pandemic decided to go do something different and got a job with the biggest online delivery company on Earth. Unlike his previous job, the new job is very physical as he is on his feet for upwards of ten hours, four days a week.

Initially, my neighbor almost resigned due to the strenuous nature of the new job but his family inspired him to stay on. After 90 days at the job, my neighbor has lost almost 20 pounds (something he has been struggling to achieve in the past five years without success), health insurance (including vision and dental), 401k (with employer's 50% match), and option to own the company's stock. My neighbor was able to achieve all these benefits (which were not available in his prior job) because he was willing to step out of his comfort zone.

Some months back, I was inspired by my first son (Ina) to venture into options trading in the Stock Market. Since then, I have continued to develop my skill by reading a lot about options / industry news generally and with constant brainstorming with my second son (Uba) who is using his computer skills to develop projections models in option trading. Option helps you to leverage on your finances by giving you a dealing control over 100 shares with limited amount of funds that would not be possible in the traditional stock market trading.

Today, this new venture is keeping my brain busy now in retirement as I strive to develop more skills in this endeavor.

THE SEVENTH BAD HABIT:
THE UNWILLINGNESS TO LEARN NEW SKILLS.

Achieving financial independence involves investments; and succeeding in investment, requires skills and knowledge. Whether you are a salaried person or self-employed, improving yourself is always a good investment. So, if you are interested in financial independence, you must learn the language of money as your financial wellbeing can only grow to the extent that you are able to grow your financial knowledge.

For instance, for business owners, investing in knowing more about your customers is key to the success of your business. So, is like learning new skills in investment opportunities, a rewarding investment for everyone who desires financial independence.

Luckily today you can obtain almost every information you need with the tip of your finger and your phone. The famous Inspirational Speaker, Anthony Robbins once said that "early in life, I developed the belief that leaders are readers. Books could take me to other lands where I could meet unique people like Abraham Lincoln or Ralph Waldo whom I could utilize as my personal coaches". In my own case, I was able to meet Robert Kiyosaki in the early 1990s through his book-Rich Dad Poor Dad- and that greatly inspired me.

Decide Today to start learning the grammar of investment by reading inspirational books on Financial Independence. The more familiar you are with financial knowledge and terminology, the more comfortable and confident you will be in participating in the investment process.

For more detailed information in starting your journey to financial freedom, kindly click the links below:

http://www.xulonpress.com/bookstore/bookdetail.php?PB_ISBN=9781615791071

https://www.amazon.com/FINANCIAL-INDEPENDENCE-AGBAI-INA-OBASI/dp/1615791078

Finally, I leave you with a summary of a paper that I presented based on my book and titled:

Inspiring our Youth to Think & Act to Achieve Financial Independence (FI):

(A) BACKGROUND INFORMATION
i) FINANCIAL INDEPENDENCE (FI)
 "Financial Independence is like a three-legged stool resting on Savings, Insurance and Investments".
ii) DREAM:
>FI begins with a dream. The bigger your dream, the better.
> Desire fervently to achieve the dream.
> The more passionate you desire, the better.
> After the dream, you must wake up to set a goal to achieve the dream.

iii) GOAL:

> Recommended that the Goal be in writing.
> The goal must be specific, measurable, challenging, and achievable- not too low and not too high.
> The important thing to note here is the passion with which the goal is set and pursued.
> Without passion, your pursuit for FI will be like the seed planted among thorns. Your success will be hindered by distractions.
> The goal must be pursued with consistency, focus and determination. > I recommend that it be shared with loved ones for effective buy in and support and avoid divergent goals.

iv) FAMILY:

> Spouses with divergent goals find it difficult to achieve FI as one spouse will want to live by the day, above their means and be happy when they spend money they have not earned.

> While the order spouse will want to save and invest in assets today that will support their future expenditure.
> FI is easily achieved when both spouses support same FI goal.
> Families are encouraged to start teaching their young ones early in their lives.

v) ACTION THE GOAL:

> After setting the goal, you must action the goal.
> This entails taking specific steps to achieve the set goal.
> Most times, this will involve CHANGE, UNCERTAINTY AND RISK.
> But remember, every breakthrough in life has come with a change.
> Such changes involve getting away from ones' Comfort Zone which is not always easy to do.
> However, nothing good ever come easy. As a guide, you can start by attaching Pain to Failure and Joy to Success of the goal you are trying to achieve. The more effective you do this, the better chances of success in actioning your goal.
> Always remember NO RISK NO INCOME. Taking risk could be deciding to work part time today to enable you go back to school for a higher degree or investing substantial part of your savings on an investment project with no guarantees.

With this Background Facts, we can now dive into the various investment opportunities.

(B) INVESTMENT OPPORTUNITY:

1) INSURANCE:

> There is no better way to protect your assets and loved ones against unforeseen circumstances than Insurance - Health, Life, Home, Car, College etc. Insurance reduces financial risk and give support when the unexpected event happens.

> The need for Insurance cannot be overemphasized for the following:

-An unexpected illness may cost a fortune without health Insurance.

-Losses due to natural disaster, accident or burglary may be expensive to replace.

-Loss of loved one is more painful and complicated by bills without life insurance.

> Therefore, Insurance is highly recommended because MAYHEM is everywhere.

The more traditional investment option is the second option – savings.

2) SAVINGS:

> The Richest Man in Babylon prescribed that we save at least 10% of our earnings. Babylon is in the current day Baghdad destroyed around 612 BC.

> Please note that What is important here is developing the habit of savings.

> Many hide behind the excuse of low wages not to save. However, it has been proven repeatedly that with determination, you can save notwithstanding your income size.

> But note also that savings alone is insufficient because of the low interest rate on savings. Therefore, you must invest those savings in a more profitable investments to be FI.

>Two areas to invest your savings are ROTH IRA which gives you tax advantage for your savings and the interest accruals; AND the TARGET INVESTMENT FUND which gives you " a complete retirement portfolio in a single fund based on the age you would like to retire.

> Remember, if you can't save, no matter how much you earn, you will never achieve FI.

From Savings, we move to the Riskier Options.

3) Stocks:

> To successfully invest in stocks, you need information on the company, the management, the trend in the company and in the industry that you would like to invest in.

> You must also know about some calculations like simple and compound interest, ROI/ROE, EPS, Etc.

> And understand some Stock Market technical words like capital appreciation, dividends, script and bonus issues, bear & bull, Initial Public Offer (IPO).

> Example Twitter was listed on NYSE at a price of $26 and closed at $46 on first day of trading; an increase of over 70% in one day in November 2013. Saving's interest is at a max of 2% PA. Compare that with 70% in one day.

> Must have an exit strategy.

> Its always advisable to use the services of a professional stockbroker or investment analysts to guide you especially at the initial time.

Tips To Investing in The Stock Market:

- Invest long time. The longer your term, the lower your risk. A minimum of 5 years Is recommended.

-Do not sell your stock immediately after a downturn to partake in the rebound.

-Don't put all your eggs in one basket. Stacy Johnson recommends subtracting your age from 100 and putting no more than the resulting percentage of your long-term savings in Stock. E.g., if you are 40 years, you can only invest 60% of your long-term savings in stock. Also, balance between growth and income.

-You have the Options to invest in the Individual Company Stocks or in the Mutual Funds or both.

-Mutual Funds Lower your risks and hassle. It is a giant pool of investment either in Stock or Bond or both that is

Managed by professionals who do the buying and selling. You should avoid commission-based financial advisers and use the Fees based ones whose fees are dependent on the income you made from the investment. Mutual funds that trade on exchanges Are called Exchange Traded Fund. (ETF)

-Systematic Investment.

Recommended that you invest fixed amounts at regular intervals. E.g., monthly. So, You get to buy more when stocks are cheap and less when stocks are high or costly.

4) REAL ESTATE:

> To be financial independent, you must own your own house (Residential)

> It's even better when the house brings income into your pocket (by way of rent)

> Mortgage is Key to owning a house and achieving one of the pillars of the American dream.

What do Lenders Consider in a mortgage transaction?

- Expense to Income Ratio; 25% to 45% recommended.

-Long term debt i.e., 10 months and above cannot be more than 36% of gross monthly Income-Loan to Value Ratio.

-Above all, maintain good credit history. Borrowers with excellent credit history may be offered lower interest Rates. Review your credit history to confirm information therein before you apply.

-Managing your credit entails that you stay within your limit, pay at least the Minimum due each month and when due, and MINIMIZE your interest payment by Paying off the balance as quickly as possible.

-Use less than 30% of your total approved credit limit.

The following will guide you in calculating your credit score:

~ Payment History/default 35%

~ How much you owe 30%

~ Length of credit history 15%

~ types and mix of credits 10%

~ New credit accounts and applications 10%.

So clearly, the longer your history of making timely payments, the higher your Credit score.

Documents from Lenders:

-Obtain a written pre -qualification from the lender.

-Loan disclosure/warranties.

-Rate lock in (rates can change between when you apply and closing) Processing Disclosure

-Transfer of loan servicing disclosure.

-The Appraisal i.e., estimated value of your home.

Kinds of Mortgages:

-Fixed, where interest rates are fixed for the term of the loan.

-Variables; where interest rates usually start low and is adjusted periodically to reflect Inflation under advice to the borrower.

-TENOR could range from 5 years to 30 years. However, the shorter the tenor, the less interest you pay on the loan.

-DOWN Payment refers to the cash you pay upfront. The more down payment amount You make, the less the monthly payment and vice versa.

Sources of Mortgage Loan:

-Retail banks, Credit Unions, Mortgage Bankers, Insurance Companies

-Federal Housing Adm. (FHA), Veterans Adm (VA), and other State sponsored Programs to help the poor and first-time buyers.

The Mortgage Agreement: (must be read in detail)
-Loan Amount
-Cost of the loan i.e., Interest charges etc.
-Repayment terms i.e., tenor, periodic payments etc.
-Default clause and consequences.

Mortgage Advantages
-Auto savings otherwise known as Equity built up.
-Refinance option which allows you to take part of the equity to finance other Investments.
-Allows you to buy a house which otherwise you could not afford at the time of Purchase.
-Tax subsidies ranging in amounts depending on your tax brackets.
-Capital gains tax exclusion on a sale of primary home for at least 2 of the previous 5 years for the first $250,000.

> Closing
-Before closing, the buyer should do the last inspection of the property and fund His/her account for the closing.
-Buyer should Respond to the Lender's request for further information usually to reconfirm the buyer's ratios before closing.
-On closing day, money is distributed to the lender, the seller and the Attorney And documents signed, and transfer of title effected
-Remember that the major payments at closing are done with bank or cashier's Checks.

Remember to consider the LOCATION and engage the services of professionals- real estate Agents, Attorneys etc. as documentation relating to land must be in writing under the law.

5) YOUR OWN BUSINESS:

> This is one of the most challenging and at the same time, the most rewarding of the investment options and involves a lot of time.
> 50% businesses fail within the first five years of their existence.
> Therefore, to own your own business:

-You must consider its impact on you and your family
-Seek support of Family, Advisors, Attorney, Accountant, Banker etc.in choosing the type of business and its funding.
-You must research on the business, type, location, name availability, permit etc.
-Review the funding options, order, and review your credit report and determine How much credit your business will need.
-Find a gap in the market to be filled and fill it with service at the appropriate price.
-Know what competition is doing and evaluate them.
-Do your business plan, cost, and projections.
-Grow your income and if you cannot, you must cut cost and reinvest you Profit.
-Know how to reach and delight your customers.
-Above all, grow your PASSION in the business as passion is the key to driving your business.
Customer is key to the success of any business; so, work hard to retain them by doing the following:
-Acknowledge customers by name in all communication.
-Keep relationship with customers simple e.g., handwritten thank you letters go a long way.

-Create customer service culture (CSC), Document CSC expectation, Track Customer service performance and Recognize, Reward and Sanction employee accordingly.

-Stay close to customers after sales using Internet, follow up and resolve issues.

Use technology to enhance your efficiency despite its cost:

-Financial management software helps track sales, expenses, and receivables, monitor Inventory purchases, and pay roll, manage cash flow, etc.

-Customer relationship management (CRM) software provides you customer Data, minimize sales and arresting costs, and helps customer retention.

-Use online and mobile banking to manage and monitor your account 24/7.

-Use website and online marketing to create awareness of your products, create and engage customers.

-Apply cloud computing for information storage and to facilitate file sharing etc.

THE ABIRIBA EXPERIENCE:

In Southeastern Nigeria, the Abiriba man is a famous entrepreneur known for his shrewdness in managing his business. However, in the past decade, as the business environment changed, many of our people were unable to change along with the times. What happened?

> Many were stuck to their lines of business ignorant of the changing business environment and skills.

> Some invested wrongly in non-income yielding assets.

> A few were outright extravagant living well above their incomes.

> Others were over leveraged and got smothered by the high cost of fund and bank charges.

> Some were ignorant of the ever-changing government policies.

< While some others just refused to move on to other businesses or to reinvest and /or diversify their investments.

I keep asking myself " how can a man who had 2 to 3 apartment buildings in Aba end up being a tenant in the same city when he could have stopped importation at some point along the line to become a landlord?" Notwithstanding the above, some gallant sons and daughters of Abiriba have kept faith with the rules and ethics of business, constantly renewing their business skills and diversifying their investments, and thereby continuously contributing towards making Abiriba retain its "Small London" status.

6) RECOMMENDED RETIREMENT GOALS FOR THE DIFFERENT STAGES OF LIFE:

> Age 25 - 35 years.

Save and Invest 30% of your income towards retirement and take advantage of employer sponsored 401(k) or start an individual retirement account (IRA).

> Age 35 - 55 years.

Save and invest 10 to 20 % of your income towards retirement. Begin to diversify your investment portfolio- bonds and income yielding investments. Apply the systematic investment approach i.e., regular periodic investment.

> Age 55 - Retirement.

Gradually shift to fixed income securities to achieve a better balance between growth and income e.g., income mutual funds, bond funds and annuities.

> After Retirement.

Regularly Review your portfolio and reallocate your investment bearing in mind your livelihood income requirement.

Retirement Tips.

    -Take full advantage of your company retirement savings plans.

    -Do not sell your stock immediately after a downturn.

    -Do not borrow from your 401(k) except on emergency.

-Have a good estimation of the cost and length of your retirement to guide you in your plan and expenditure while in retirement.

7) TAKE ACTION:

> Develop yourself (knowledge is key; without it, my people perish).
> Think positive, Seek God's favors.
> Act today on one thing you believe can aid you to be financially independent.
> Remember, FI is never thought in school. The earlier you start you and your young ones on it, the better.

> Finally, the best way to start is to read inspirational book on Financial Independence. "Early in life, I developed the belief that Leaders are Readers. Book could take me to other lands where I could meet unique people like Abraham Lincoln or Raph Waldo Emerson whom I could utilize as my personal coaches" ... Anthony Robbins.

With this quote, I end my presentation.

Thank you.

Agbai Ina Obasi
Author: Financial Independence.

Conclusion

TAKE ACTION

Finally, after reading this book, even if you do nothing else, I urge you to think positive, seek God's favor and TAKE ACTION today on one thing you believe can aid you to be financially independent in the nearest future.

> Ultimately, in order for a change to last,
> we must link pain to our old behavior
> and pleasure to our new behavior
> and condition it until its consistent —
> what you link to pain and pleasure
> will shape your destiny.
>
> -Anthony Robbins

TAKING ACTION involves developing yourself (knowledge is key; without it, my people perish), thinking positive, and seeking God's favors. Remember, financial independence is never thought in school. The earlier you start yourself and/or your young ones on it, the better.

Finally, the best way to start is to read inspirational book on Financial Independence. "Early in life, I developed the belief that Leaders are Readers. Book could take me to other lands where I could meet unique people like Abraham Lincoln or Ralph Waldo Emerson whom I could utilize as my personal coaches" ... Anthony Robbins.

With this quote, I end.

BIBLIOGRAPHY

Clason George; The Richest Man in Babylon. Published by Signet an Imprint of New American Library a division of Penguin Putnam Inc. 375 Hudson St New York [1988]

Jackson Adam J; The Secrets of Abundant Happiness. Published by Harper Collins Publishers San Francisco [1995]

Fisher Mark; The Instant Millionaire. Published by New World Library 58 Paul Drive California [1990]

Blanchard Kenneth Ph. D and Johnson Spencer MD; The one-minute Manager. Published by Berkley Publishing group, a division of Penguin Putnam [1981]

Robbins Anthony; Awaken the Giant within. Published by [Fireside books] Simon and Schuster Inc New York [1981]

Tharp Van K; Trade your way to Financial Success. Published by McGraw Hill Publishers [1999]

Johnson Spencer, Roberts Tony, and Blanchard Kenneth; Who moved my cheese? Published by G.P Putnam's Sons a member of Penguin Putnam Inc375 Hudson St New York 1998

ABOUT THE BOOK

Many people go through life broke because of their inability to understand their finances. Consequently, they suffer humiliations, impoverishment, and loss of self-esteem. They end up short- changing themselves and loved ones. All that would
have been avoided, IF ONLY THEY KNEW.

This book deals with various investment options illustrated with real life experiences. It is my little contribution towards equipping our people by sharing my experiences and valuable wealth creating lessons that I have learned over the years.

I believe that as you read this book, you will be inspired by it to Think, Act, and achieve financial independent.

ABOUT THE AUTHOR

Agbai Ina Obasi obtained a BA degree in Public Policy Administration in 1983 from Lakeland College, Sheboygan, WI and a Juris Doctorate (JD) in Law in 1986 from Marquette University Law School, Milwaukee, WI, USA.

He spent thirty years in the Financial Industry with more than twenty one years in the banking sector where he rose to a position of GM/CEO of a bank subsidiary in Lagos, Nigeria.

Agbai is a Notary Public, a licensed Insurance Producer in the great state of North Carolina, the author of three published books, and an e- book titled, "Seven Bad Habits that Inhibits Achievement of Financial Growth".

He is now retired but still active in online Option Trading and with his writings, always aimed at inspiring the youth to Think and Act to achieve financial Independence.

Agbai is happily married to his beautiful wife-Chinyere Obasi and blessed with three lovely grown children- Ina, Nnenna and Uba.